019749

DISCARDED

BUILDING A NATION

LIFE IN THE
THIRTEEN COLONIES
1650-1750

Written by:
Stuart Kallen

LIFE IN THE THIRTEEN COLONIES

Published by Abdo & Daughters, 6535 Cecilia Circle, Edina, Minnesota 55439

Library bound edition distributed by Rockbottom Books, Pentagon Tower, P.O. Box 36036, Minneapolis, Minnesota 55435

Library of Congress Number: 90-082617   ISBN: 0-939179-87-3

Cover Illustrations by: Marlene Kallen
Inside Photos by: Bettmann Archive

Cover Illustrations by: Marlene Kallen
Edited by: Rosemary Wallner

TABLE OF CONTENTS

CHAPTER 1
THE THIRTEEN COLONIES

They Called Themselves Americans

By the 1650's, over fifty thousand settlers from Europe were living in the New World. By 1750, over one million people lived in the New World. These settlers no longer considered themselves English, Italian, Spanish or French. They had made the new world their home; they were a new breed of people. They called themselves Americans. The Native American Indians who had lived in America had been killed in wars or had moved west. Some lived among the white men.

Hundreds of new settlers arrived from Europe every day, most of them from England. These people came to America with dreams. They dreamed of wealth and religious freedom. Many dreamed of owning their own land, something that was impossible for most people in the crowded cities of Europe.

In the early 1600's the Europeans lived in a handful of scattered settlements in the American wilderness. But by the 1650's, these settlements had grown into towns. Some of the towns had grown into bustling cities. Soon America was divided into thirteen colonies. The colonies were what we would now call states. The people that lived in the colonies were called colonists.

Three Different Life Styles

When the colonists put down roots in America, they developed different ways of living depending on their location. Each colony had its own life styles depending on the ruggedness of the land and climate. The thirteen colonies were divided into three areas where trade and farming were similar. These regions were: the New England Colonies of Massachusetts, Rhode Island, Connecticut and New Hampshire; the Middle Colonies of New York, New Jersey, Pennsylvania and Delaware; and the Southern Colonies of Virginia, Maryland, North Carolina, South Carolina and Georgia.

Between 1650 and 1750 North American colonies developed into three regions: the New England Colonies, the Middle Colonies, and the Southern Colonies. Life in each area was distinctive. According to this map, which colonies made up each section?

The Thirteen Colonies, 1750

MAINE (PART OF MASS.)

NEW HAMPSHIRE

Boston

NEW YORK

MASSACHUSETTS

Providence

Hartford

RHODE ISLAND

CONNECTICUT

New York

NEW JERSEY

PENNSYLVANIA

Philadelphia

DELAWARE

MARYLAND

Baltimore

Jamestown

VIRGINIA

NORTH CAROLINA

SOUTH CAROLINA

GEORGIA

ATLANTIC OCEAN

New England Colonies

Middle Colonies

Southern Colonies

0   400 Miles

0   600 Kilometers

CHAPTER 2
THE NEW ENGLAND COLONIES

Against the Odds

New England is known for its harsh winters. Violent storms leave heavy snowfalls. High winds and bitterly cold temperatures freeze rivers for months. The colonists from England were not used to such frigid weather.

If that was not enough to discourage even the most hardy settlers, the rugged landscape did. The topsoil was thin and not too fertile. The dirt was peppered with rocks that had been left by glaciers during the Ice Age. Along the coast lay a vast no-man's-land of sand dunes and saltwater marshes. Inland, thick, overgown forests had to be cleared for farming. Cutting down those forests by hand was backbreaking labor.

But there were rewards for the hardworking colonist. Any person with a boat and a fishing rod could feed his or her hungry family on the rich bounty of the coastal waters. Timber and furbearing animals were plentiful and very valuable in the cities.

Massachusetts

For thousands of years, the Algonquian Native Americans lived near a huge hill in what is now Boston. They called their home Mes-atsu-s-et which means *large hill place.* When the Pilgrims arrived in the area in 1620, they adopted the name and called their new home Massachusetts.

By the 1650's, thousands of people had come to Massachusetts. Most of these colonists practiced the Puritan religion. The Puritans settled the areas on the coast of the Atlantic Ocean. Soon the towns of Boston and Salem were thriving. As the populations of these cities grew, more and more people traveled west into the wilderness to build their own cities. Boston was soon surrounded by the cities of Lexington, Concord, Springfield and Worcester. All of Massachusetts was governed by the rules set forth by the Puritan church.

The Puritans had been forced out of England because of their religious beliefs. They had traveled to America in order to practice their religion without interference from the government. Once in America, however, the Puritans forced everyone who was living in Massachusetts to practice Puritanism. From the 1630's until the end of the century, all the people living in Massachusetts had to live under the strict Puritan rules. By the 1700's, the king of England revoked the Puritan Charter and more liberal and tolerant behavior was allowed.

Rhode Island

In the early 1600's, Adriaen Block, a Dutch sea captain, made a note in his journal about a place that had "fiery red clay" on its shores. His Dutch name for it was Roodt Eylandt, which means "red island." When the English pronounced it "Rhode Island," the name stuck.

Rhode Island was settled by people who were driven out of Massachusetts for disagreeing with the Puritans. People in Massachusetts who did not follow the Puritan rules were whipped, jailed and even executed.

One man who disagreed with the Puritan church was Roger Williams. Williams was a Puritan minister who spoke out against the many church rules. He believed the church should be separate from the government.

On a bitterly cold day in January 1636, in the midst of a snowstorm, the Puritan governors forced Roger Williams to leave Massachusetts.

The Native Americans greet Roger Williams.

Leaving behind his wife and children, Williams walked alone through the snowy woods until he came upon a Native American village. The people welcomed Williams and took care of him for several months.

When the winter turned to spring, Williams brought his family and a few followers to the shores of Narragansett Bay of Providence, which is today the capital of Rhode Island. Williams knew that the land belonged to the Narragansett tribe. Unlike the Puritans, who simply forced the Native Americans off of the land, Williams bought the land for a fair price.

Another person who was forced to leave Massachusetts by the Puritans was Anne Hutchinson. In 1637, Hutchinson was brought to trial for challenging Puritan rules and refusing to fight the Pequot tribe. After defending herself bravely at the trial, Hutchinson was forced to leave Massachusetts with her husband, their fourteen children and seventy-three supporters. The Hutchinsons went to Rhode Island and founded the city of Portsmouth.

Rhode Island was the first colony where people could practice any religion they chose. That idea would later become the foundation of American freedom.

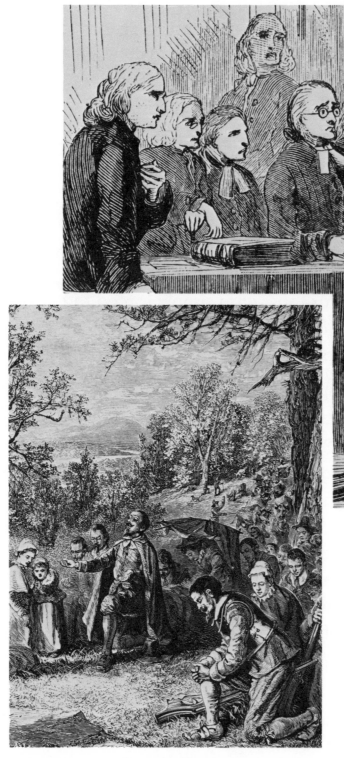

Thomas Hooker.

Connecticut

Connecticut is another state that got its name from the Algonquian Native Americans. The Algonquians called the main river in the area the Kw-Eniht-Ekot meaning "long tidal river." The English changed the spelling to Connecticut.

Connecticut was colonized by another unhappy Puritan minister, Thomas Hooker. He disagreed with the Puritans over the issue of voting. In Massachusetts only Puritan men were allowed to vote. Hooker believed that all white men should be allowed to vote, no matter what their religion.

In the summer of 1636, Hooker and one hundred followers left Massachusetts for the fertile valley of the Connecticut River. After weeks of walking with their wagons and farm animals, they finally found a perfect spot to build a town. They named the city Hartford and today it is the capital of Connecticut.

Several years later, the 800 people living in the colony drew up a set of rules to govern themselves by. They called the rules the "Fundamental Orders of Connecticut." This was the first written plan for government of any of the colonies. The plan also guaranteed the right to vote to white men of any religion.

Connecticut was also the sight of the first large-scale battle between the Native Americans and the settlers. In 1636, a Pequot Native American attacked a troublemaking white trader. The Puritans used the attack as an excuse to burn tribal villages and crops, and massacre hundreds of Native American men, women and children. That incident started a war between the white men and the New England tribes that would last for the next one hundred years. This was a war that the Native Americans would eventually lose. In the early 1600's, tens of thousands of Native Americans lived in New England. By 1760, only several hundred were left.

Maine, Vermont and New Hampshire

The fishing grounds, farmland and forests north of Massachusetts were a powerful attraction to many new settlers. Thousands of colonists went to the wild woodlands of Maine, Vermont and New Hampshire. At first these colonies were part of Massachusetts. In 1679, the English king gave settlers permission to start the colony of New Hampshire. Vermont was a part of Massachusetts until 1791, Maine until 1820.

CHAPTER 3
LIFE IN THE NEW ENGLAND COLONIES

Down on the Farm

Gathering berries. Collecting maple syrup. Making brooms. Taking care of farm animals. These were just some of the chores that were given to children in colonial New England. When children were not doing chores, they studied religion and schoolwork.

In spite of the poor soil in New England, most people earned a living as farmers. Most grew just enough to feed their families and had very little left over for profit. Some farmers used African slaves, but most farms were too little and too poor to use slave labor.

Once a family picked out their farm land, the hard work began. First, the trees were cut down, and the wood was used to build a house, barns, and tools that the farmer would need. Next, all the rocks had to be removed from the soil so that the farmer could plant his crops. The fieldstone were used to build walls around the farm.

After the land was cleared, the farm family planted corn, rye, peas, carrots, squash, pumpkins and other hardy vegetables. The farmers also kept chickens, sheep, cows and pigs so that they had a steady supply of meat, cheese, wool, milk and eggs.

Every member of the family helped in the farm work. Men did most of the planting and hunting. The women made clothes, candles and soap, pounded corn into meal, preserved the vegetables and meat and took care of the cooking. Children were expected to help as soon as they could walk.

The Community
The center of a New England community was the Puritan church. Since Sunday services lasted all day and the shortest sermon was two hours, some churches locked their doors so that no one could leave. During the middle of the day, the minister would stop talking, and everyone would gather for lunch. The families ate and talked with their neighbors and then returned to church for the rest of the day.

An illustration of Boston by Paul Revere.

The members of each village would help each other out. If a family's crops failed, neighbors would share extra food. The men would help each other build barns and harvest crops. Sharing helped the struggling towns survive.

Big Cities

Life in a large New England city like Boston was quite different from life on the farm. People in the cities depended on trade with England and with the other colonies for their needs.

In the early days, trapping furs was a good way to make money. Europeans were clamoring for American beaver, raccoon and otter furs for coats, hats and gloves. Unfortunately, the trappers were so skillful that by the 1670's all the animals in the area had been killed.

The rich forests provided many jobs for the colonists. The lumber industry became a major source of income for the region.

Down to the Sea in Ships

Because of the vast hardwood forests, New England became the center for the shipbuilding industry. Boston alone boasted twelve shipyards. The New England ports had over nine hundred oceangoing vessels and five thousand fishermen.

Fur trappers weighing furs to be sold.

Besides fish, huge whales made the New England waters their home. Because whale oil was burned in lamps and whale bone was used for jewelry, whales were hunted to near extinction.

New England became the center of trade between England, America and the islands of the West Indies. New England's shipping trade brought people from all over the world to her sandy shores. The shipping trade also brought huge sums of money to New England cities and towns.

Witchcraft in Salem

To the strict, religious Puritans of New England, the Devil was a constant threat. The Puritans feared that the Devil was hiding in every closet and behind every barn to steal the soul of a nonbeliever. The Puritans were always ready to do battle with the Devil and his servants, witches.

The fear of witches had been brought to America from Europe. There, tales of witches were as common as stories of elves and fairies. The cry of "witch" had been heard throughout early American history. In 1692, the accusations got out of hand.

In that year, Reverend Samuel Parris of Salem, Massachusetts, employed a black servant named Tituba. The neighborhood children loved Tituba because she taught them how to meow like kittens and bark like dogs.

A young girl accuses a Puritan woman during a Salem witch trial.

One day, eleven-year-old Abigail Williams had some spasms in church. She told the preacher that a yellow bird was sitting on his hat. Her playmates, Anne Putnam, Mary Walcott and others also acted strangely. Fearing the preacher, the girls said that they had been bewitched by Tituba and two old women, Sarah Good and Sara Osborn.

Judges, ministers and sheriffs rounded up the accused and held a trial based on the ravings of the terrified young girls. After the women were jailed, the girls started to accuse other people in Salem of witchcraft. Soon, people settled arguments and ruined the lives of their enemies by falsely accusing them of witchcraft.

People invented stories of three-foot-tall creatures covered with hair, spirits sliding through keyholes and men conversing with the Devil. Hysteria swept through the colony.

Before the madness had run its course, 150 people had been thrown in jail, one victim had been crushed to death under a pile of stones, and 19 men and women had been hanged. All had been falsely accused of witchcraft.

CHAPTER 4
THE MIDDLE COLONIES

The English Take Over
In 1664, King Charles II ruled England. His brother James, Duke of York, sailed his warships to New Amsterdam, the Dutch city on Manhattan Island in present-day New York City. Because the people of New Amsterdam were tired of being ruled by the Dutch, they surrendered to James without a fight. The island and all of the Dutch holdings in America became the property of the English king. The lands included all of present-day Pennsylvania, New York, New Jersey and Delaware. The British added these areas to their growing number of American colonies.

New York
Thirty-eight years before the English took over New York, Dutchman Peter Minuit had purchased Manhattan Island from the local Native Americans for twenty-four dollars. There, the Dutch had built the city of New Amsterdam. After James, Duke of York, obtained the lands for England, he changed the name of the city and all the lands west of it to New York after his hometown in England.

King Charles II, Ruler of England.

While New England grew at a steady rate, New York's growth was slow. Large amounts of land along the Hudson River were owned by a few wealthy Dutchman known as *patroons*. These patroons sometimes controlled hundreds of thousands of acres of land. They charged farmers rent and taxes. A portion of the farmers' crops were also paid to the patroons. Because most farmers would not put up with such conditions, few settled in the area.

Another reason why New York's growth lagged behind the other colonies was more serious. The French claimed the land in much of northern New York and were willing to fight to keep it. The Iroquois tribe had lived in New York for over fifteen centuries, and they too were willing to fight to keep their land.

New Jersey

When James took all of the lands from the Dutch, he also gained the vast amount of land from the Connecticut River to Delaware Bay. But the cost of governing all that land was too much for the king's brother. After several months, James gave the land between the Hudson River and the

James II, Duke of York.

Admiral William Penn.

Delaware River to his friends Lord John Berkeley and Sir George Carteret. They named their colony New Jersey after the Channel Islands of Jersey in England.

Lord Berkeley and Sir Carteret offered land to settlers for low prices. They also offered the colonists the right to govern themselves. Thousands of people came from Scotland, Ireland, France, Germany, the West Indies and New England to settle New Jersey.

Soon the colony was thriving. The warm climate and fertile soil made the land ideal for growing wheat, corn, oats and other grains. Flour mills used river waterpower to grind the grain into flour. New Jersey became the supplier of bread to the other colonies.

Because of its close location to New York City, New Jersey grew and prospered by supplying the city with lumber, food and services.

Pennsylvania

When King Charles II of England was in trouble, Admiral William Penn had lent him a large sum of money. When Penn died, King Charles repaid the debt to his son who was also named William Penn. Even though the land belonged to the Native Americans, Charles II gave a huge tract of land to the younger Penn and named it Pennsylvania, which means "Penn's woods."

The king accomplished two goals by giving the land to Penn. Not only did he pay off a debt by giving away something that did not really belong to him, but he also got rid of Penn and his religious group, the Quakers.

The Quakers had gotten their name because their founder had directed them to "quake and tremble at the name of the Lord." The English rulers did not like the Quakers. The Quakers treated everyone as equals and refused to fight in wars. In the 1600's, Quakers in England and Massachusetts were sent to prison and even executed for their religious beliefs. William Penn decided to use Pennsylvania as a place where Quakers could worship without fear of persecution.

Since there were not enough Quakers in England to build a colony, Penn advertised all over Europe for people to come to Pennsylvania. The promise of peace and equality inspired people to pack up their belongings and head for Pennsylvania. Soon Pennsylvania was populated with people from Scotland, Ireland, Germany and Sweden. Pennsylvania's fertile soil helped to make its farmers the most successful in America.

The bustling city of Philadelphia.

The City of Brotherly Love

In 1682, William Penn sailed up the Delaware River with 200 Quaker colonists. Penn built a city on the river and named it Philadelphia, which means "the city of brotherly love" in Greek. Because the Quakers believed in equality and respect for all human beings, thousands of people came to Philadelphia. Penn also showed respect to the Native Americans in the Pennsylvania area by paying them for the land that the king had given to him.

By 1750, Philadelphia was the largest city in America. The city's docks were crowded with men loading and unloading ships with tobacco from Virginia, rum from the West Indies, and wheat, beef and lumber from Pennsylvania.

Near the docks a busy marketplace grew. Farmers sold their fresh milk, eggs and cheese while fishermen sold their days catch. Native Americans came to town to sell their corn, beans and furs.

Past the waterfront were all kinds of shops. Clockmasters, silversmiths, blacksmiths, printers, furniture makers and other craftsmen plied their trades. Restaurants and taverns fed the hungry workers. Soon, people from all over the world were flocking to the busy streets of Philadelphia to live the good life.

Thanks to Benjamin Franklin, Philadelphia became one of the greatest cities in America. Franklin helped to organize a police force, a fire department, postal service and paved street construction.

Delaware

In 1610, a ship commanded by Captain Samuel Argall was blown off course on its way to Virginia. Argall named the spot where he landed after Virginia's governor, Lord De La Warr. The name Delaware was later applied to the area's bay, river, Native American tribe, and colony.

In the early 1600's, Delaware was the sight of battles between Holland and Sweden, both countries claiming the land. In 1664, when the English captured New York from the Dutch, they also claimed Delaware. In 1682, the Duke of York gave Delaware to William Penn who made it part of Pennsylvania. In 1776, Delaware became a separate colony. The flat land and rich soil in Delaware made it a haven for Swedish, Dutch and Finnish farmers.

CHAPTER 5
LIFE IN THE MIDDLE COLONIES

Because of the rich soil and warm climate, the Middle Colonies were the wealthiest in the land. Religious freedom and self-government instilled pride in the people, giving them the desire to work hard to make their colonies the best in America. Since America was still mostly wild forests and untamed woodlands, many Americans lived their whole lives farming the backcountry without any interference from the government and its tax collectors.

The streets of large cities like New York and Philadelphia were colored with a rainbow of different cultures. About half of the people in the Middle Colonies were of English ancestry. But America was filling up with people from Scotland, Spain, Italy, Germany, Sweden, the West Indies, France and elsewhere. America's promise of freedom of religion brought together Catholics, Protestants, Baptists, Jews, Quakers and many other religions to live together in relative harmony.

By 1750, one out of five people in America (20 percent) were African slaves.

Though slavery was legal in the Middle Colonies, the farms were much smaller and needed less labor than in the Southern Colonies. Most Northern slaves worked as household servants and at skilled or unskilled trades in towns. Although many Africans in the North were "free," laws were passed that limited what jobs they could have and where they could live. Some black people escaped this racism by moving into the wild areas of the frontier.

CHAPTER 6
THE SOUTHERN COLONIES

The Colonies That Tobacco Built

The Southern Colonies were very different from the other colonies. The warm climate and fertile soil was ideal for growing tobacco. In the 1650's people did not know that tobacco was unhealthy to smoke. Tobacco had become very popular in Europe. Because it is addictive, the demand for tobacco grew and grew as more people started smoking it and could not quit.

Tobacco factory in the south run by slaves.

As the popularity of tobacco increased, so did the price. Many men in the Southern colonies became very wealthy growing tobacco with slave labor on huge plantations.

Virginia

Virginia was the first English colony in America. The colony was named after Queen Elizabeth I. Elizabeth was not married and was known throughout her forty-five-year reign as the Virgin Queen.

Jamestown, Virginia, was the first English settlement in North America. Virginia had the ideal soil and climate to grow tobacco. The tobacco industry changed Virginia from a starving, struggling settlement to a thriving, wealthy colony in a few short years.

Virginia was the leader of the thirteen colonies and four founding presidents of the United States (George Washington, Thomas Jefferson, James Madison and James Monroe) were born and raised there.

Maryland

The wife of England's King Charles I was named Henrietta Maria. When Charles I gave a colony to his friend Lord Baltimore he suggested that Baltimore name the colony "Mary's land" for his queen. Thus the colony was named Maryland and its first city Baltimore.

Maryland, like Virginia, was a colony of huge tobacco plantations. Because the vast waters of the Chesapeake Bay ran through the heart of Maryland, tobacco growers found it easy to load their products on ships bound for Europe.

Besides farming and tobacco, the woods in Maryland and Virginia were abundant with deer, bear, beaver and other animals valued for their fur. Many fur trappers became wealthy by trapping animals in the forests for the colony.

The Carolinas

Charles was a popular name for kings. The area known as the Carolinas was named for three different kings: King Charles IX of France and Kings Charles I and II of England. "Carol" was the feminine pronunciation of Charles. In 1712, the colony was split into two sections, North Carolina and South Carolina.

As available land for farming disappeared in Virginia, many settlers moved south to the Carolinas. These settlers were called *squatters* because they did not own the land; they just lived on it and farmed it.

When King Charles II gave the land to eight of his friends in 1663, the men, known as *proprietors* let the squatters stay on the land. The proprietors taxed the squatters and made laws for them to follow.

In 1670, seventy colonists built the settlement of Charles Town on the Ashley River. The area was low and swampy and many settlers died from diseases carried by the mosquitos that lived there. In 1680, the settlers moved to a healthier spot where the Ashley met the Cooper River. This area became the finest harbor in the South. Soon people from all over the world were moving to Charles Town. The city today is known as Charleston.

Tobacco did not grow as well in the Carolinas as it did in Virginia and Maryland. In 1740, Elizabeth Pinckney successfully grew a plant called *indigo* in the Carolinas. Indigo is a plant from the West Indies that is used to make blue dye for clothing. Planters soon started to grow this valuable crop. Cotton and rice were also big cash crops for the Carolina planters. Indigo, cotton and rice were all grown on huge plantations using slave labor.

Georgia

Georgia was the last English colony to be founded. In 1732, the land was separated from South Carolina and given to James Oglethorpe by King George II. Oglethorpe named the colony Georgia after his king.

The reasons for founding Georgia were different than for the other thirteen colonies. The other colonies were founded as either moneymaking ventures or as places for religious freedom. Georgia was founded as a place where English prisoners could pay off their debt to society. In England, if a person was too poor to pay his or her bills, the government would put that person in jail. Oglethorpe talked King George II into releasing the poor people from jail and sending them to build the colony.

Since the Spanish ruled the lands now known as Florida, Georgia was also settled as a buffer zone between Spanish Florida and the English colonies. Many battles were fought between the Spanish and English settlers on the southern Georgia border.

Oglethorpe built the city of Savannah and the colonists began to grow rice and indigo. They were soon as successful as their neighbors to the north.

CHAPTER 7
LIFE IN THE SOUTHERN COLONIES

In many ways, the landowners of the South lived like the kings and queens of European royalty. Because tobacco, rice and indigo were only profitable if grown on huge areas of land, plantations of 10,000 acres were common.

The Plantation

The heart of each plantation was the great house or mansion. There, the planter family lived in splendor. Persian rugs, fine artwork and imported furnishings filled their homes. Each mansion had a music room, a library, a ballroom, a variety of parlors, a huge dining room and kitchen and a wine cellar. Since the nearest neighbors might live one hundred miles away, each mansion had many guest rooms for friends who stayed overnight. Planters had many lavish parties.

Surrounding the mansion were a bakehouse, a stable, a dairy, a schoolhouse where a teacher lived, a blacksmith shop, a brickworks, a smokehouse, a flour mill and cabins for slaves and servants. Everything that could not be made on the plantation such as silks, books, fine furniture and some tools were imported from England.

The Planter Family

The planter family was a busy one. The landowner would decide which crops to plant and when to plant them. He would arrange for the harvest, shipping and sale of the crops. With his wife, the planter would oversee the servants, cooks, skilled craftsmen, clerks and slaves.

A typical Southern mansion.

Women's legal rights to land were limited, but the planters wife often played a large role on the plantation. Many women helped their husbands make important decisions. Supervising the huge household was a full-time task.

Many times the planter's children were sent to England to receive a proper education.

Indentured Servants

The life style of the planters could only be supported by the efforts of many people. When the plantation system was first started, planters hired people known as *indentured servants*. These men, women and children were given free passage to America if they promised to work for a planter for seven years. At the end of seven years, the indentured servant received clothing, tools, a rifle and a parcel of land and was set free.

Many servants were glad to come to America this way. Some were not. Throughout the colonial period, the English government sent boatloads of convicts and political prisoners to America. Drifters, orphans, poor people and troublemakers were often forced to be servants on plantations.

Bacon's Rebellion

Many people who were freed servants developed a hatred of their former masters because the planters had all the good land. When the servants were freed, they usually ended up in the backwoods barely able to scrape a living out of the land.

In 1676, friction between the poor farmers and the planters exploded into open warfare. When the farmers in Virginia felt that the planters had failed to protect them from the Native Americans, the farmers marched into Jamestown. Led by Nathaniel Bacon, a wealthy farmer who was on their side, the farmers burned the capital to the ground and attempted to break up the huge plantations. In the middle of the revolution, Bacon died. The uprising, known as Bacon's Rebellion, fell apart and the leaders were hanged.

Why Slavery?

Meeting labor needs with indentured servants was difficult for planters. Since servants only worked for seven years, the planter had to continually replace the work force. The skills of running the

Governor Berkeley condems the men who led Bacon's Rebellion.

plantation had to be taught to new people all the time. And there were never enough servants to meet the demand. Furthermore, the backcountry was becoming filled with unhappy former servants. Another uprising like Bacon's Rebellion could happen at anytime.

Under these conditions the demand for slave labor grew. The first Africans were brought to Jamestown in 1619. By the time the first slaves arrived in Virginia, over one million Africans had been brought as slaves to South America and the Caribbean by the Portuguese and Spanish. In 1442, fifty years before Columbus landed in the new world, the Portuguese had brought blacks to Portugal to work as slaves.

In 1672, the English started the Royal African Company to kidnap Africans and bring them to America as slaves. Slavery became a very profitable business for nearly 200 years.

The Life of a Slave
The cruel life of slavery for blacks began in their home country of Africa. In Africa, nearly 100 million people lived in many different ways. They lived in cities that were as beautiful as any in

Europe or America. Like the Native Americans, the Africans had many different tribes and languages and all manner of fantastic artwork, clothing and music.

Slave traders hunted down Africans and put them in chains. The traders marched them hundreds of miles to the coast to await shipment to America. After being put in pens for up to two weeks, the Africans were branded with hot irons and loaded on to ships.

On the slave ships, men, women and children were forced to lie, chained at the neck and foot, in spaces less than two feet high. For week after week, the slaves were kept below deck while the ship sailed across the Atlantic Ocean. As many as one third of the Africans died of suffocation, starvation and disease.

Once the surviving slaves arrived in America, they were sold to plantation owners who forced them to work at backbreaking labor in the tobacco, cotton and indigo fields. Some slaves were trained as carpenters, blacksmiths or other skilled laborers. The luckiest ones worked in the mansions as cooks, butlers, servants and nannies.

Slaves had no legal rights and were treated as property — no different than a mule or plow. Plantation owners could break up a family and sell the children of their slaves. The slaves had nowhere to escape to and were forced to give up their language, customs and religions.

By the 1800's, it is estimated that Africa lost fifty million human beings, or half her populaton, to death and slavery. Ten to fifteen million slaves lived in America.

Cotton plantations in the south used slave labor.

A Final Word

The colonists in different areas faced different challenges. But the seeds of some very special ideas were planted in the rich soil of American thought. Those ideas were growing in all thirteen colonies because things were different than in Europe. In Europe, people had been denied control over their government and had been told what religion to practice. And unless a person had a lot of money, their children could not attend school. In America, the idea of religious freedom was taking hold. Public schools and a government elected by the people were also new ideas that were growing in the New World. Between 1650 and 1750, ideas spread throughout the land that would one day be written as law in the American Constitution.

INDEX